Spectacular Sports

World's Toughest Races

Understanding Fractions

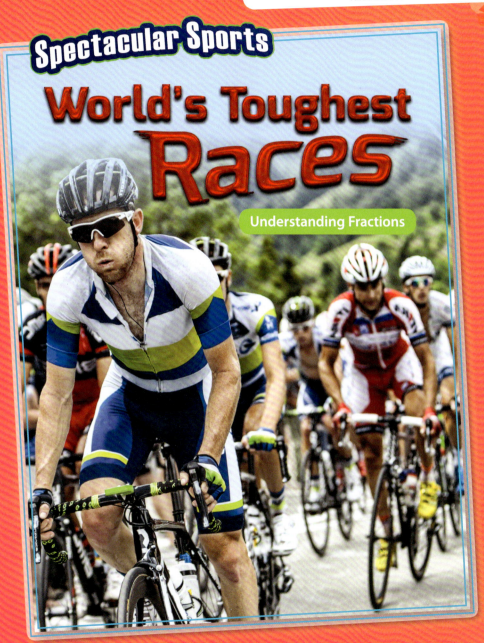

Saskia Lacey

Consultants

Michele Ogden, Ed.D
Principal, Irvine Unified School District

Jennifer Robertson, M.A.Ed.
Teacher, Huntington Beach City School District

Publishing Credits

Rachelle Cracchiolo, M.S.Ed., *Publisher*
Conni Medina, M.A.Ed., *Managing Editor*
Dona Herweck Rice, *Series Developer*
Emily R. Smith, M.A.Ed., *Series Developer*
Diana Kenney, M.A.Ed., NBCT, *Content Director*
Stacy Monsman, M.A., *Editor*
Kevin Panter, *Graphic Designer*

Image Credits: pp. 4-5, 12-13 Courtesy Thom Gilligan of Marathon Tours & Travel; p. 6 Photograph by Alakananda Lebedeva; pp. 8, 9 David McNew/Getty Images; pp. 10, 11 Alexander Beer/ZUMA Press/Newscom; p. 13 INB Wenn Photos/Newscom; pp. 14 (top and bottom), 14-15 Martin Bernetti/AFP/Getty Images; p. 17 D. Ross Cameron/MCT/Newscom; p.22 (bottom) epa european pressphoto agency b.v./Alamy Stock Photo; pp. 22-23 Olivier Pojzman/ZUMA Press/Newscom; p. 23 (top) Olivier Pojzman/ZUMA Press/Newscom; p. 25 LAPI/Roger Viollet/Getty Images; all other images from iStock and/or Shutterstock.

References Cited: Gray, Will. 2012. "Interview with Nick Gracie of Team Adidas TERREX/Prunesco." SleepMonsters Ltd. http://www.sleepmonsters.com/v2_races.php?article_id=7503
McIntosh, Amanda. 2011. "Lessons Learned at Badwater." Badwater University. http://www.badwater.com/university/lessons-learned-at-badwater/
Windsor, Richard. 2016. "Chris Froome: 'Before counts for nothing. I'm hungrier than ever for success.'" Cycling Weekly. http://www.cyclingweekly.co.uk/news/racing/tour-de-france/chris-froome-counts-nothing-im-hungrier-ever-success-234616

Library of Congress Cataloging-in-Publication Data

Names: Lacey, Saskia.
Title: Spectacular sports : world's toughest races / Saskia Lacey.
Other titles: World's toughest races
Description: Huntington Beach, CA : Teacher Created Materials, [2017] | Audience: K to grade 3. | Includes index.
Identifiers: LCCN 2016053333 (print) | LCCN 2017008289 (ebook) | ISBN 9781480758025 (pbk.) | ISBN 9781480758667 (eBook)
Subjects: LCSH: Racing--Juvenile literature. | Fractions--Juvenile literature.
Classification: LCC GV1018 .L34 2017 (print) | LCC GV1018 (ebook) | DDC 796--dc23
LC record available at https://lccn.loc.gov/2016053333

Teacher Created Materials

5301 Oceanus Drive
Huntington Beach, CA 92649-1030
http://www.tcmpub.com

ISBN 978-1-4807-5802-5

© 2018 Teacher Created Materials, Inc.
Printed in China WAI002

Table of Contents

Built to Be Brutal 4

Outrageous Obstacle Courses 18

Bike Across Borders 22

Dream Big 27

Problem Solving 28

Glossary 30

Index 31

Answer Key 32

Built to Be Brutal

The world of racing is changing. Courses are longer. Their settings are more extreme. Obstacles are stranger and more dangerous. Athletes want to try things that seem impossible. They want a chance to prove their strength.

So, races are created. Obstacles are built. Incredible courses are designed to test the strongest of the strong. Athletes train hard. They need to be ready for icy **terrains**, desert winds, and steep climbs. They must have superhuman endurance.

These races are built to be **brutal**. They are not for everyday athletes. Only serious competitors need apply. You may have heard of some of these races, but you probably don't know them all. Have you ever heard of the Antarctica Marathon? What about the Jungle Marathon? Does the Tough Mudder® ring any bells? Each has its own difficulties. All are super tough. Which is the toughest? You be the judge.

Athletes make their way through the Antarctica Marathon course.

Contestants compete in the Beaver Run, Lithuania's version of the Tough Mudder obstacle course.

Tough Around the World

The first course seems simple. Racers do not face weird hurdles. There are no wild locations. The weather is not extreme. In this race, there is just one city block. Easy, right? Well…maybe not.

The Self-**Transcendence** (tran-SEN-dents) 3100 Race takes place every year in Queens, New York. The race is 3,100 miles (5,000 kilometers) long. That is like running all the way across the United States! And, there is one more challenge. Runners have to finish the race within 52 days. Athletes must run almost 60 mi. (100 km) a day to finish on time.

It may seem impossible. But, the athletes who finish have a lot to brag about. It is the longest footrace in the world!

Many runners don't want to just finish the race. They want to beat the record. In 2015, the winner finished in just 40 days, 9 hours. He had to run a little over 76 mi. (122 km) each day.

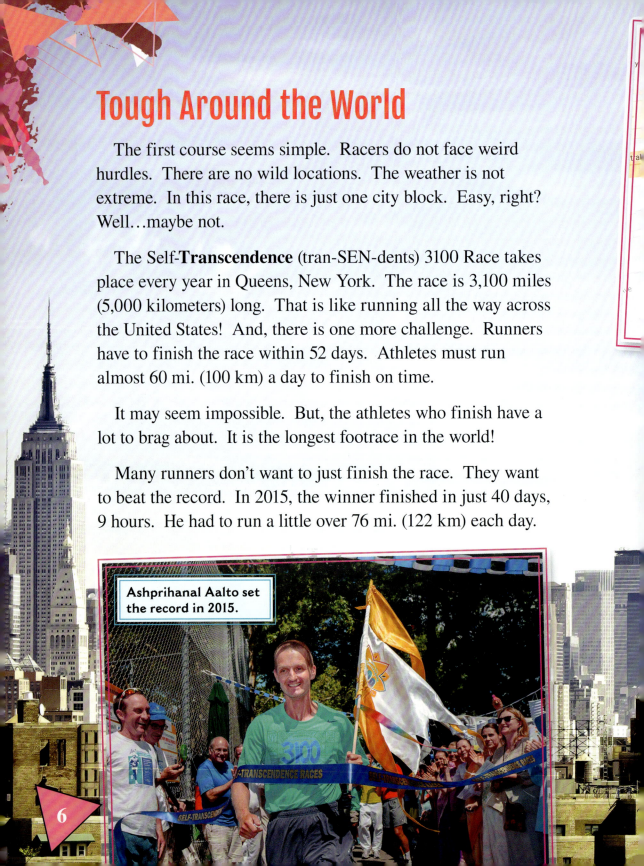

Ashprihanal Aalto set the record in 2015.

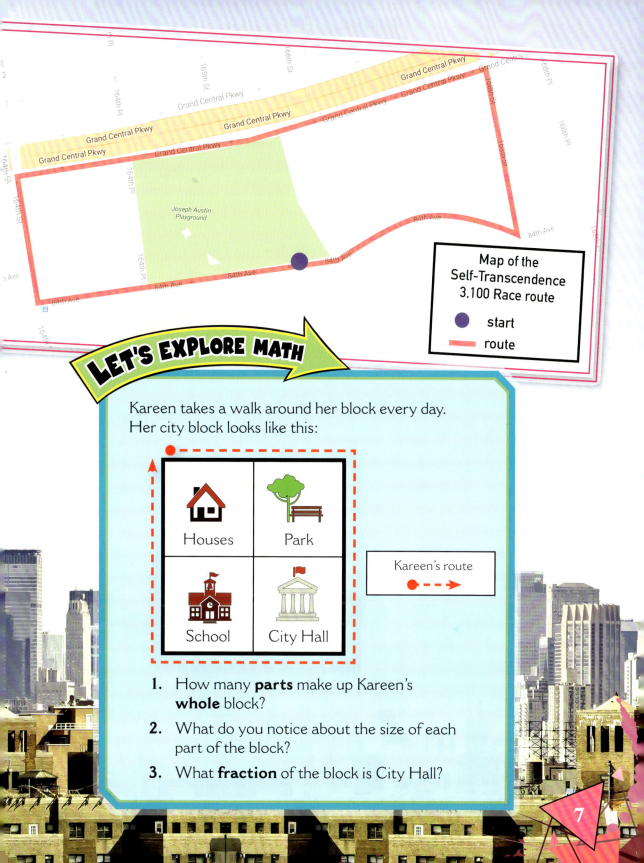

LET'S EXPLORE MATH

Kareen takes a walk around her block every day. Her city block looks like this:

1. How many **parts** make up Kareen's **whole** block?

2. What do you notice about the size of each part of the block?

3. What **fraction** of the block is City Hall?

Badwater® 135

The Badwater 135 is not an easy race. Runners travel 135 mi. (217 km) through the Death Valley desert in July. If you're thinking about running, then be sure to bring plenty of water! Death Valley lives up to its name. It is the hottest place on Earth. To make it to the finish line, racers have crews that help them stay calm and cool. The crews follow the runners as they race. They make sure runners keep going. They also help keep them safe.

One crewmember, Amanda McIntosh, was worried about the heat. "When I stepped out of the van, it was like jumping into an oven." But by the end of the race, Amanda was almost a **convert**. "While I still **contend** that this is not a race for me…I now understand the **allure** of Badwater." The racers impressed her. She was amazed by how they pushed past the intense heat.

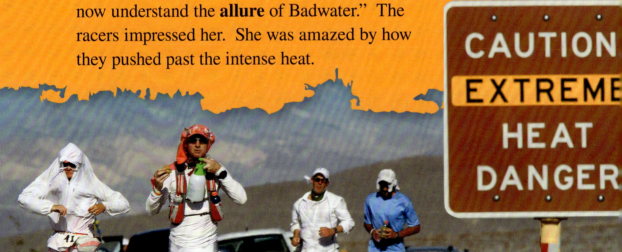

Runners try to stay cool in the extreme heat.

A crewmember squeezes wet sponges over a runner's head.

LET'S EXPLORE MATH

Crewmembers at the Badwater 135 carry extra bottles of water and ice to hand to the runners. The water that is left in one runner's bottle is shaded on the model.

1. Does the water bottle have more or less than half remaining?

2. What fraction of the water in the bottle does the runner have left?

3. What fraction of the water in the bottle did the runner already drink?

Josie Benson competes in the 2014 Jungle Marathon and places first among female competitors.

Marathon through the Amazon

The Jungle Marathon is one of the toughest races in the world. It takes place in the Amazon jungle. It is hot, humid, and very dangerous. Runners have to **endure** temperatures over 100 degrees Fahrenheit (40 degrees Celsius). So, don't try this race if you are scared to sweat!

It's not just heat that makes this race tough. The course is over 150 mi. (240 km) long. Athletes must survive in the wild. They must build shelters and live off the land. They have to be ready and aware at all times. Danger lurks in every corner. There is plenty to be wary of in the jungle. There are big predators. Anacondas and jaguars lurk in the jungle. There are insects that bite and sting. Creatures like tarantulas crawl underfoot.

This race may not be easy, but the payoff is huge. Runners are not just in it for a medal. They also want to experience the untamed beauty of the Amazon.

jaguar

pink-toed tarantula

Antarctica Marathon

If the Jungle Marathon sounds too hot for you, you may want to check out the Antarctica Marathon. Biting winds hit runners along the way. **Subzero** temperatures are common. But, runners prepare for this. After all, it is in Antarctica—the coldest place on Earth!

This icy race is a standard marathon—a little over 26 mi. (42 km). But, this race is anything but standard. It takes great skill to be able to run through the freezing cold.

A pack of runners start their adventure on the Antarctica Marathon.

Winter Vinecki is one of those skilled racers. When she was just 14 years old, she ran the Antarctica Marathon. She finished the race in less than 5 hours. This is a big deal for any age!

But Winter did not stop there. She set a goal to run a marathon on every continent. And she did! Winter was the youngest racer to do this.

Winter Vinecki

A French team suits up for this adventure in endurance.

The M.O.B. (Mind Over Body) team from Canada takes on the mountain biking portion of the race.

Patagonian Expedition Race

The Patagonian (pa-tuh-GOH-nyuhn) Expedition Race is famous for its beauty. There are mountains and plains. There are glaciers and deserts. You name it, this race has it! Athletes on the course feel lucky. Not many people get to see the wonders of this area up close.

Training for this race can be like a guessing game. Each year, the course changes. Athletes are never sure what will be around the corner. But, they *can* be sure that their bodies will be pushed. Teams of four must work together to climb, run, bike, and kayak to the finish line.

The route is revealed 24 hours before the race begins. Athletes must be able to think on their feet. Every decision is a way to get ahead or fall behind.

One of the course's greatest athletes is Nick Gracie. His team has won four times! Gracie says that when people ask him where they should travel, his answer is always the same: Chilean Patagonia. Gracie says, "It's the most beautiful place I've ever been on the planet."

The U.S. team kayaks through southern Chilean Patagonia.

Fierce Frisco

The San Francisco Ultramarathon® is a little over 52 mi. (84 km) long. That is the length of two marathons! Athletes start racing at midnight and keep running through the next day. The course is not easy. San Francisco has tough terrain. There are many steep hills. Even the strongest athletes are nervous to run the race.

To qualify as a finisher, athletes must run the nighttime part of the race in five hours or less. Then, they have to run the daytime part of the race in six hours or less. This is part of the reason why so many of the runners keep running through their **fatigue**. One more step feels like one too many. But, they keep going because it is an honor to run the course.

The race is limited to only 100 of the best athletes. Each of these runners competes for a cause. By racing, they will raise money for the charity of their choice. Their legs will get weak. Their lungs will burn. But these ultra-athletes keep fighting their way to the finish line.

Ultramarathon runners start the race before dawn.

LET'S EXPLORE MATH

Enzo is running a mile on a course.

1. Enzo started at 0 on the course. What fraction of a mile has Enzo already run?

2. What fraction of a mile does Enzo still need to run if he wants to run a whole mile?

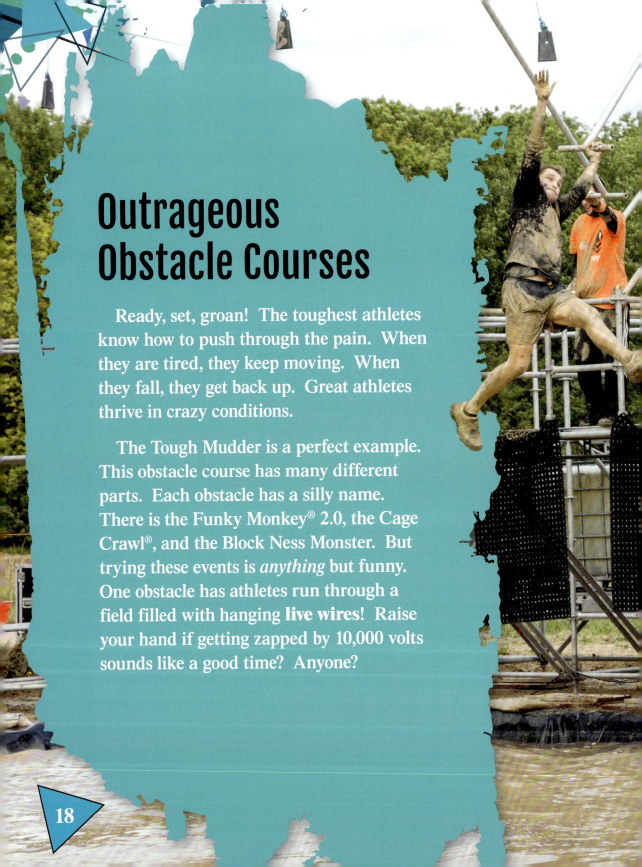

Outrageous Obstacle Courses

Ready, set, groan! The toughest athletes know how to push through the pain. When they are tired, they keep moving. When they fall, they get back up. Great athletes thrive in crazy conditions.

The Tough Mudder is a perfect example. This obstacle course has many different parts. Each obstacle has a silly name. There is the Funky Monkey® 2.0, the Cage Crawl®, and the Block Ness Monster. But trying these events is *anything* but funny. One obstacle has athletes run through a field filled with hanging **live wires**! Raise your hand if getting zapped by 10,000 volts sounds like a good time? Anyone?

Tough Mudder athletes try to reach the bell without falling into the water.

LET'S EXPLORE MATH

Elise is planning an obstacle course in the circular field next to her school. Even though the course won't be as extreme as the Tough Mudder, it is sure to be fun for her and her friends!

1. How many parts make up the whole obstacle course?
2. What do you notice about the size of each part of the obstacle course?
3. What fraction of the obstacle course is being used for hopscotch?

An athlete emerges from the Sewer Rat obstacle.

With a puff of orange smoke, runners set out to conquer the Tough Mudder.

But live wires are just one of the Tough Mudder's terrors. There are also obstacles with extreme temperatures. One features a dumpster filled with freezing water. Wading through pounds of ice is a teeth-chattering task. Some athletes choose to test the waters before they jump in—big mistake. The only way to make it through this ice-cold challenge is to take the plunge. The same can be said for most of the Tough Mudder's crazy obstacles.

In recent years, the Tough Mudder has introduced new races. Now, there is The World's Toughest Mudder®, a 24-hour race without a finish line. The course is 5 mi. (8 km) long. It is filled with every obstacle you can imagine. And, racers don't just run the course once. They run it over and over. The athlete who runs the course the most times in a day, wins.

An athlete leaps over the Fire Walker obstacle.

Bike Across Borders

Some athletes prefer to race on two wheels rather than on two feet. Every year, some of the world's best cyclists put their pedals to the test and compete in Race Across America. The course goes from California to Maryland. Cyclists may compete alone or in teams. Most cycling contests have scheduled rest days. But, Race Across America does not. This makes it harder to compete alone. Cyclists on teams can spend less time riding and more time resting. This is helpful as they bike from coast to coast.

But, the distance is not the only challenge. Athletes must complete the race in just 12 days. That means they must ride about 250 mi. (400 km) every day. That is some serious mileage! Most people don't even like to drive that far in a day. Imagine what it must be like on a bike!

The best cyclists only rest for about 90 minutes each day. The rest of the time they ride. How is this possible? Perhaps only Race Across America cyclists will ever know!

RACE ACROSS AMERICA
OCEANSIDE, CA TO ANNAPOLIS, MD · 3000 MILES

A support crew vehicle follows a racer.

Cyclists start the race in Oceanside, California.

23

Le Tour de France®

Le Tour de France is a race with a long history. It takes place over many weeks. Cyclists cover thousands of miles. They ride through many countries. For over 100 years, athletes have fought to win the famous race. All of them want to wear the yellow jersey given to the winner.

The first race was in the summer of 1903. It started and ended in Paris. There were 60 competitors. Fast forward to 2016. Nearly 200 cyclists competed. What a difference 100 years makes!

In 2016, Chris Froome won Le Tour de France for the third time. The champion is still excited about racing. Froome believes that cyclists start as equals each year. He says, "What has gone before counts for nothing. This year I am hungrier than ever for success." These are the words of a committed athlete.

Chris Froome completes a time trial wearing the famous yellow jersey.

Let's Explore Math

Cyclists racing in Le Tour de France represent many countries. Teams wear similar jerseys. Each team wants to win!

Take a look at the graphic below. Cyclists are wearing three colors.

1. What fraction of the cyclists are in red?
2. What fraction of the cyclists are in blue?
3. What fraction of the cyclists are not in yellow?

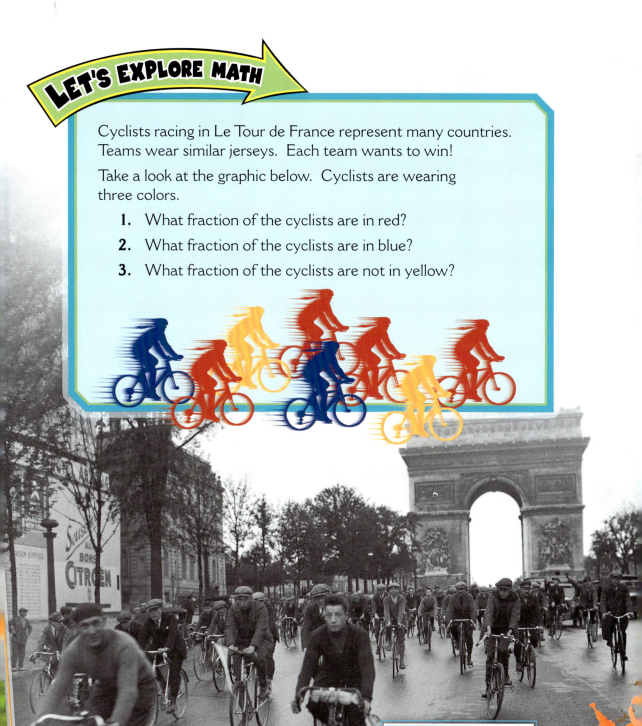

Athletes race through Paris in 1926.

These young athletes race in the 2-km Kids Run at the Laguna Phuket International Marathon™ in Thailand.

A family wades through a water obstacle during a mud run event.

Dream Big

Athletes train for years before competing in the world's toughest races. These are extreme courses. They are designed to inspire the toughest athletes from around the world. From Paris to Patagonia, top-level athletes test their skills. One thing all of the athletes have in common is their drive to compete.

But, even the best athletes have to start somewhere! Do you have what it takes to compete in one of these races? You just might! Explore races near you. You'll find that there are races for athletes of all experience levels. Or, maybe you just want to take a walk around the block. All that matters is that you lace up your shoes and go!

Problem Solving

Taj and his friends love to ride bikes. But, they aren't quite ready for the **grueling** Le Tour de France. So, they have started their own race, Le Tour de Park! It's not Le Tour de France, but they have fun just the same. Their course is 1 km long through the park, with markers along the way. Just like the riders of Le Tour de France, Taj and his friends each want to be the winner! Use the clues to plot Taj and his friends at their current points in the race on the number line. Then, answer the questions.

1. Who is closer to the $\frac{4}{8}$ marker on the course: Dora or Jen?

2. Is Ben closer to the $\frac{4}{8}$ marker or the finish line? How do you know?

Clues

- Taj is at the $\frac{4}{8}$ marker.
- Ada is $\frac{6}{8}$ of the way from the finish line.
- Sean is at the $\frac{1}{8}$ marker.
- Dora is $\frac{6}{8}$ of the way to the finish line.
- Jen is $\frac{3}{8}$ of the way to the finish line.
- Ben is $\frac{1}{8}$ of the way from the finish line.

1 km Course

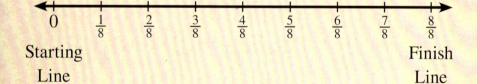

Starting Line   Finish Line

Glossary

allure—power to attract or influence someone

brutal—extremely violent or difficult

contend—to claim or state

convert—someone who has changed their beliefs

endure—to continue past pain or unpleasantness

fatigue—the state of being extremely tired or exhausted

fraction—a number that shows how many equal parts are in a whole and how many of those parts are being described

grueling—very difficult or requiring a lot of effort

live wires—wires that carry an electrical current

parts—pieces that make up a whole

subzero—below 0°F (–18°C)

terrains—certain kinds of land

transcendence—existence beyond normal experience

whole—having all the parts; complete or full

Answer Key

Let's Explore Math

page 7:
1. 4 parts
2. Each part is the same size.
3. $\frac{1}{4}$ of the block

page 9:
1. less than half
2. $\frac{2}{6}$ (or $\frac{1}{3}$)
3. $\frac{4}{6}$ (or $\frac{2}{3}$)

page 17:
1. $\frac{3}{8}$ of a mile
2. $\frac{5}{8}$ of a mile

page 19:
1. 3 parts
2. Each part is the same size.
3. $\frac{1}{3}$ of the obstacle course

page 25:
1. $\frac{4}{8}$ (or $\frac{1}{2}$) are in red.
2. $\frac{2}{8}$ (or $\frac{1}{4}$) are in blue.
3. $\frac{6}{8}$ (or $\frac{3}{4}$) are not in yellow.

Problem Solving

Number lines should show Taj at $\frac{4}{8}$, Ada at $\frac{2}{8}$, Sean at $\frac{1}{8}$, Dora at $\frac{6}{8}$, Jen at $\frac{3}{8}$, and Ben at $\frac{7}{8}$.

1. Jen is closer to the $\frac{4}{8}$ marker.
2. Ben is closer to the finish line. He is $\frac{1}{8}$ km away from the finish line and $\frac{3}{8}$ km away from the $\frac{4}{8}$ marker.

Index

Antarctica Marathon, 4, 12–13

Badwater 135, 8–9

Froome, Chris, 24

Jungle Marathon, 4, 11

McIntosh, Amanda, 8

Patagonian Expedition Race, 15

Race Across America, 22

San Francisco Ultramarathon, 16

Self-Transcendence 3100 Race, 6

Tough Mudder, 4, 18–19, 21

Tour de France, Le, 24–25, 28

Vinecki, Winter, 13

World's Toughest Mudder, 21